BOOKED TO THE GILLS

Booked to the Gills

to the Gills

How to Crush Thirty-Day
Writing Challenges for Busy People

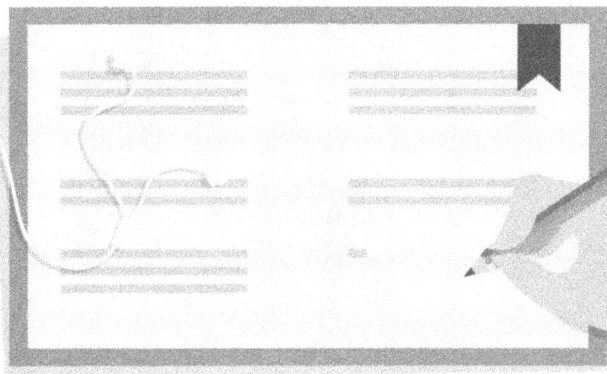

Aisley Oliphant

Booked to the Gills:
How to Crush Thirty-Day Writing Challenges for Busy
People

Copyright © 2022 by Aisley Oliphant

eBook ISBN: 979-8-9869032-1-7
Paperback ISBN: 979-8-9869032-0-0

Cover Design by MiblArt
Star Chart Photograph by Jessica Sedgwick
Published by VariantWorks Publishing House, LLC
721 North Main Street, #345
Layton, UT 84041

First Edition: September 2022

For my fellow Jedi Masters...
Love you guys.

"A rising publisher lifts all books."

CONTENTS

INTRODUCTION

"You don't have to be [insane] to do this…
but it helps."
—moonsword27, National Novel Writing Month
Forums, Oct 2009[1]

The happiest accident that ever happened to me was
the day I got the wrong order at Nielson's Frozen
Custard. Normally, I would have returned to ask if I
could get it fixed, but the long drive-thru line,
packed interior, and proximity to closing convinced
me my go-to hot fudge sundae wasn't worth it. So, I
decided to live with it.

And oh boy… I'm glad I did.

The order I received was a Nielson's chocolate
Concrete with mini peanut butter cups and smooth

peanut butter swirl. The cold, creamy custard and crisp, candy crack zapped tingles from my tongue to brain at the first bite. Whoever invented this combo was a custard connoisseur, a visionary, a frozen dessert fiend!

I've not gone back to my old order since.

My second happiest accident was almost as enigmatic. It was November 21, 2020… the day I realized I had completed National Novel Writing Month™ in eighteen days while learning to work from home, worrying about a surging pandemic, dealing with the loss of loved ones, managing friend and family relationships, and so much more. It was an all-around, much-needed success amidst a crappy time in history.

But looking back at the experience, I realized there wasn't as much "accident" to my win as I had thought there was. There was a method underneath that I had been developing over many, many years of participation. It only took a burst of success to see it.

National Novel Writing Month (aka NaNoWriMo™) is one of my favorite writing challenges, but it can be incredibly difficult to finish. Every November, writers around the world choose to participate in a challenge to write a 50,000-word novel in only thirty days. This feat requires the participant to write a minimum of 1,666 words per day in order to cross the 50,000-word mark before midnight on November 30th and thus be considered a "winner."

Out of the eight years I've participated in the challenge so far, I have won six times. Each win (and loss) taught me something new and helped me refine a strategy that allows me to manage work, school, hobbies, family obligations, and other relationships, and still secure a win at the end of November. NaNoWriMo 2019 was particularly pivotal, as I discovered a strategy that allowed me to hit those 50,000 words in twenty-one days while balancing a full-time day job, two hours of commuting, family obligations, and active membership in two writing groups. Then, in that fateful November of 2020, that same strategy allowed me to finish in a record eighteen days while still juggling a job, family and friend relationships, writing groups, and self-care to combat the mental and emotional effects of the pandemic.

Now, don't panic. I know that writing 50,000 words in thirty days sounds nearly impossible and extremely daunting. And if you're anything like me, you absolutely DO NOT have the time. As writers, we are painfully familiar with balancing the oppressive weight of deadlines and with the behemoth of work that already hangs over us. It seems impossible to cram in words as it is with work, school, family, extracurricular activities, and any number of other obligations—our time is too often booked to the gills.

But I have good news.

We have more time than we think.

Time management expert Laura Vanderkam said in her October 2016 TED talk[2] that, "Time is highly elastic. We cannot make more time, but time will stretch to accommodate what we choose to put into it."

Winning challenges like National Novel Writing Month isn't just about writing as many words as you possibly can. It's about planning *how* you are going to fit those words into your schedule. As Vanderkam asserts, your time will expand to fit what you choose to put into it, and as long as you are intentional about when you get your writing done, the rest of your obligations will fall into place, even if you are incredibly busy. I want to show you how to reverse engineer your time so you can win National Novel Writing Month and similar events with the time you have by using time blocking, accountability, catch-up strategies, and realistic expectations, goals, and boundaries.

I understand that everyone's circumstances are different and not everyone has an interest in competing in writing challenges. However, I believe these tools can be applied across the board, no matter the project. Because I developed these strategies over the course of National Novel Writing Month, I will be teaching in terms of the competition, but feel free to apply them to your own situation as you see fit.

CHAPTER 1
TIME BLOCKING

"Time is what we want most, but what, alas! we use worst."

—William Penn, *Fruits of Solitude*, 1682[1]

Have you ever wanted something so bad, you didn't care what consequences you reaped while chasing it? You know, the kind of bad where you let bridges burn, grades slip, and stayed up so late you went about your day in a haze?

It's a special kind of drive for sure (the masochistic kind, to be honest), but this was how badly I wanted to win National Novel Writing Month in 2012. Up to that point, I had participated in the challenge twice, once unofficially and once officially. I failed miserably both times. But, like a lot of us who want to be writers when we grow up, I'd been dreaming of finishing my first full manuscript since I was a child.

This time, I was determined to do it.

I prepared by spreading the news. My family was a little skeptical, but mainly because they had watched me squirrel from idea to idea without finishing anything for *years*. But they didn't push back or express non-support. Telling my creative writing professor, however, was a different story.

I distinctly remember telling her I planned to write a novel in a month, and she looked at me like I was crazy. She didn't think I could do it and was worried about the impact it would have on my classes if I tried. But I shrugged and told her I was determined. The conversation left very much on a "Okay, prove me wrong" note, but I didn't care. I was going to win.

At the beginning of the challenge, I did fairly well. I got close to the daily word counts, writing more words in a day than I had ever before. I kept pushing just a little harder until I *finally* hit the cumulative word count needed on day six. In the background, I managed to stay on top of my assignments and enjoy the process of strengthening my writing muscle.

I remained either a little ahead or right on target for the next three days... and then week two struck like a viper.

For someone who was used to writing a hundred words here and there whenever the muse called, writing a couple thousand words per day was unsustainable. I just didn't have the muscle for it. Sure, I had pulled the occasional all-nighter to write term papers, but this was like writing a term paper *every night*. It was so stressful to keep up while also balancing my homework and my part-time job.

My word counts suffered, and so did everything else.

I started staying up so late, I would write in my sleep. I'd be cranky the next day and snap at my family. I stopped hanging out with friends. I got behind on my homework, like my professor feared. I spent the month walking around in the aforementioned stress- and frustration-induced haze. Before I knew it, the evening of the last day arrived, and with it, the realization I was behind over 11,000 words... and had *two hours* left to finish.

I took drastic measures.

Locking myself in the backseat of my parents' car

where I wouldn't have any distractions or keep anyone awake with my keyboard or lights, I blasted Two Steps from Hell through my headphones and typed the fastest I ever had in my life.

The words I wrote that night were absolute garbage and hardly made sense. I jumped from scene to scene like a maniac, the tendons in my wrist on fire. I pushed through tears and prayed that I'd cross the finish line and complete a book for once in my life.

One minute before midnight on November 30, 2012, I pasted my manuscript into the NaNoWriMo word count verifying software and won by the skin of my teeth at 50,688 words.

Looking back at this experience, I can see the mistakes I made that led up to that stressful dumpster fire of a win, the biggest being my inability to make time in my busy schedule to write. Sure, yeah, I didn't have the writing muscle either, but I know if I had better managed my time, I wouldn't have had so many words to write in those final two hours.

This is one of the most common barriers I've seen for people choosing to do NaNoWriMo. Squeezing those extra minutes out of the day can feel daunting and impossible, and many people aren't sure how to do it (I sure didn't). However, the trick to finding the time is recognizing where your time gets spent. Creating a calendar of what you do in a day makes it easy to see when you have gaps to fit in a few words. One of the best methods of time visualization is a productivity technique called *time blocking.*

WHAT IS TIME BLOCKING AND WHAT IS IT USED FOR?

Time blocking is a time management strategy in which you block out your calendar to focus on specific to-do list items. These could be external appointments, household chores, answering emails, or relaxation time. The purpose of this is to help you devote all of your focus to one task or group of similar tasks at a time, thereby increasing your productivity by reducing distraction or multitasking. It also helps you be more realistic about the availability in your day, as well as help you see where you are wasting time.

I tend to plan my daily schedule this way, but if needed, you have the flexibility to time block for weekdays or months at a time. Instances in which you may want to consider blocking weekdays or months could include sanctioning administration days in the work week, arranging a monthly editorial calendar, or creating a homeschooling schedule, however for the purposes of winning NaNoWriMo, I have found hour by hour daily planning to be the most effective as it helps me find pockets of time for writing.

A CRASH COURSE IN TIME BLOCKING

The first thing you'll need is a calendar or planner of your choice. I prefer to use Google Calendar because it is easy to move appointments, change their length, and color code them, but you can use Microsoft Outlook, a bound planner, a piece of paper—really anything that will allow you to visualize your time.

Next, make sure your obligations are up to date in your calendar. Add in things like meetings, practices, classes—anything that has a fixed time slot and that other people are counting on you for. For example, my family usually schedules family pictures in November, so when I'm planning for National Novel Writing Month, I find out when that is and schedule accordingly. Be sure to sanction time to get ready and travel as you are filling out your obligations, keeping in mind to reserve a little extra to account for snags like traffic, fussy kids, lost keys, etc.

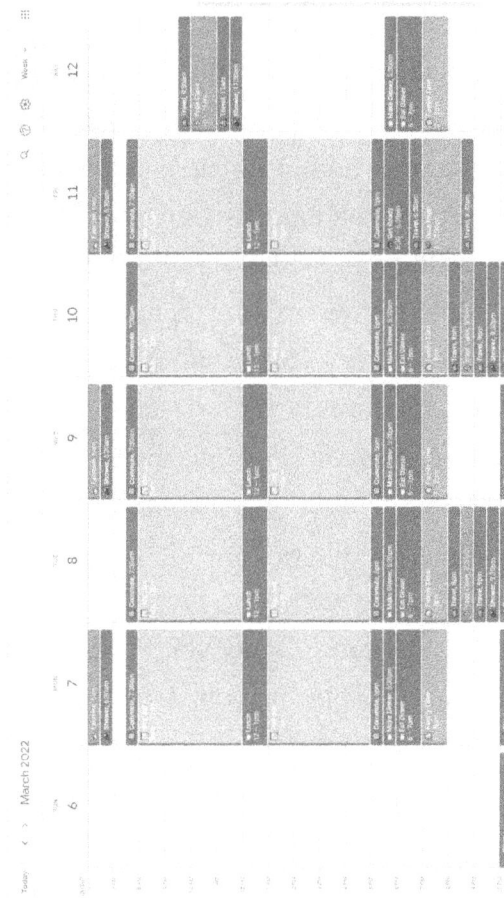

An example of a best-case scenario, time blocked calendar. Digital image available at www. aisleyoliphant.com/booked-to-the-gills-example-calendars.

Now that your solid obligations are in your calendar, you can add in your more flexible ones. For me, flexible obligations are things like when I'm going to exercise, run errands, or cook dinner. For those with children, it could be one-on-one play or quality time. Or, those with demanding jobs could plan in relaxation time. This category includes whatever obligations you need to keep your life running, but the world won't end if it is done at a different time every day or week. It is important to note that because these items can (and probably will) be moved around, it can be hard to predict when you'll be able to do them or how long they will take, so as you are planning, focus on *best* case scenarios and *approximate* time limits for how long tasks will take you.

To illustrate this, let's say you are someone who has an 8 am to 5 pm day job, a commute, a small family, and a weekly yoga class. On your calendar, you would drop in the solid appointments first, which in this case are the expected work hours and the yoga class. Afterward, you would lock down space before and after those slots to accommodate for commute time, prep time, shower time, etc. Last, you would schedule those more flexible, but important items, like date night, family time, and unstructured workouts.

Once you have all your obligations, both solid and flexible, inserted into your calendar or planning tool of choice, you are ready to start blocking in that writing time!

USE TIME BLOCKING TO PLAN YOUR MONTH

Planning your writing appointments for National Novel Writing Month becomes easier when you see what is consuming your time and how much of your day or week remains unplanned. The following steps will help you evaluate when to write and how much work you will need to complete each session to win NaNoWriMo with the time you have.

STEP 1: PLAN YOUR WRITING

Take a look at all the open slots you have after inputting your external obligations in your calendar. When could you fit a writing session? You can take this step a day or a week at a time, but I like to look at the whole month to start. This way, I can see if I have a time that is open every day, like my lunch hour at work, and schedule a recurring calendar appointment for it. I like to get in as many recurring sessions as possible before I move down to the weekly or daily level so that when I plan session word counts, I can edit the whole series, rather than a hundred smaller appointments.

In the example from the previous section, planning in the flexible and solid obligations reveals a considerable amount of white space, much of it at consistent times. The mornings where no workouts are planned, writing can be done instead. Most evenings are left open and free for drafting as well. Saturdays also appear to have lots of space, so creative time can be booked whenever your brain works best. And lunches could be cut down to a half an hour with the remaining time available for NaNoWriMo use.

But what if your calendar is so varied, it is hard to find any one, consistent time to write? Get those blocks of time planned when you can. Focus on best case scenarios and don't commit yourself to a "minimum" writing time. I used to think that if I didn't have thirty to sixty minutes available to write, it wasn't worth sitting down to do it. However, I've learned a five or ten-minute writing session has the power to give you that last push over the finish line at the end of NaNoWriMo. Don't count any scrap time out!

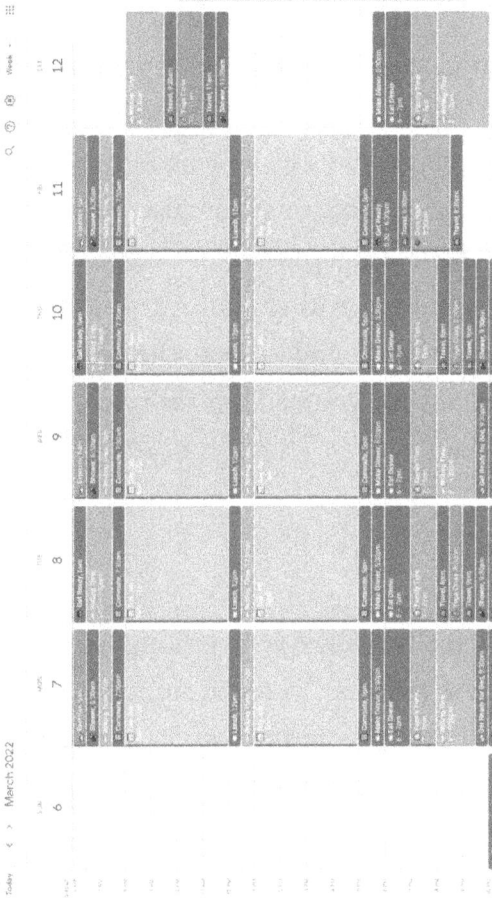

An example calendar with writing sessions filled in. Digital image available at www. aisleyoliphant.com/booked-to-the-gills-example-calendars.

Bear in mind that things will come up, as things often do. This schedule you are building is *not* law and should not be so rigid you have no room to breathe. It is okay to move writing sessions to accommodate emergencies or surprises; but, do your best to keep these appointments with yourself. Make sure the items you are moving your work for are truly important and are not excuses to avoid writing. If you are finding yourself looking for reasons to cancel or move writing sessions, you may need to take a step back and assess whether or not your expectations for yourself are realistic. More on that in Part Four.

STEP 2: TAKE STOCK

Now that you have your writing sessions blocked out on the calendar, you can sum up the total time you have available and determine how fast you will need to write to finish within it.

Start by adding up the blocks of time you set for all your writing sessions. After you know how many hours you have available for writing, use the following equations to calculate how many words per minute you will need to write in order to finish National Novel Writing Month on time.

$$50,000 \text{ words} \div X \text{ hours} = Y \text{ words per hour (wph)}$$

Replace $\mathscr{X}$ with your available hours to get Y, and then plug the words per hour you calculated for Y into the second equation to get the required typing speed.

$$Y \ wph \div 60 \ minutes = Z \ words \ per \ minute \ (wpm)$$

Let's say, for example, I have 100 accumulated hours available in November to participate in NaNoWriMo. I replace $\mathscr{X}$ with 100 to get 500 words per hour, like so:

$$50,000 \ words \div 100 \ hours = 500 \ wph$$

After, I replace Y with 500 words per hour in the second equation and divide it by 60 to get 8.33 words per minute. When I'm left with a decimal for words per minute, I always round up to give myself a buffer:

$$500 \ wph \div 60 \ minutes = \sim 9 \ wpm$$

So, in this case, I know I'll need to write nine words per minute in order to win! Keep this number handy as you are going to need it to figure out your target word count for each of your writing sessions.

STEP 3: CALCULATE WORDS NEEDED PER WRITING SESSION

The next step entails figuring out how many words you need to write every session blocked on your calendar. This number is going to vary per session, so if you have a lot of little chunks, you will need to do the math for each one.

To figure out how many words you will need to write per session, use the following equation:

$$X \text{ minutes} \times Y \text{ wpm} = Z \text{ words for session}$$

Substitute your writing session minutes for X, your needed words per minute for Y, then multiply them to get Z, the number of words you need to write in that session.

To use my previous example, if I wanted to calculate how many words I needed to write in a half hour session at nine words per minute, all I would do is multiply nine by thirty and voilà! I know I need to write 270 words that session to stay on track!

$$30 \text{ minutes} \times 9 \text{ wpm} = 270 \text{ words for session}$$

Do this step for each session block to get actionable goals and prepare for Step 4.

STEP 4: INSERT WORD COUNTS INTO YOUR CALENDAR

With your session word counts close at hand, turn to your calendar for the whole of November. Go into each session and plug your target number of words per session into the title of the appointment for the whole month.

🖊 🗑 ✉ ⋮ ✕

⚙ ▪▬· Writing Time (270 words)
Wednesday, March 9 · 12:30 – 1:00pm
Weekly on weekdays

📅 Writing
    Created by: Aisley Oliphant

*An example of a word count inserted into a
Google Calendar appointment.*

I do this in my Google Calendar because the moment I get the reminder for an upcoming writing session, I know what my target will be and how long I have to hit it. The idea of writing 50,000 words in a month is much more manageable when it is broken down into smaller chunks.

Having all this information in the title of your appointments gives you a roadmap; however, in order to *win* National Novel Writing Month, you will need more than just a visual representation of the work ahead. Seeing how your time is spent is critical to helping you know where you're going, but keeping yourself accountable for the words you write is *how* you get there. Without an accountability strategy in place, it will be much harder to make it to the finish line.

CHAPTER 2
ACCOUNTABILITY

"At the end of the day we are accountable to
ourselves—our success is a result of what we do."
—Catherine Pulsifer[1]

Accountability is key to succeeding in National Novel Writing Month. You need clear insight into the work you are doing and the progress you are making to help you stay on track for writing 50,000 words in thirty days. Pearson's Law, coined by world-renowned statistician Karl Pearson, illustrates the need for accountability this way:

"When performance is measured, performance improves. When performance is measured and reported, the rate of improvement accelerates."[2]

This means that when we are consistently tracking our progress and reporting back to ourselves, we are more likely to see how far we have come and get motivated to keep going. It also helps us see the places we could improve and educates the plans we create to facilitate growth. In turn, this helps us get better, faster.

The first time I learned about National Novel Writing Month, I was a sophomore in high school. I'd heard about it online and remembered thinking to myself, "Huh. That sounds fun and hard." I decided I would give it a go just for kicks.

I have no records of how well I did. I didn't register through the website, and I didn't keep track of my word count or stay accountable to anyone. I just… did more work than I normally would on my project at the time. The most I did to record my progress was print off the ten pages I wrote that month and staple them into my project notebook.

It wasn't until 2011 that I decided to try again and "officially" participate. I don't remember the experience, but my data shows I was not committed. I updated my word count intermittently and then flatlined the rest of the month. But my experience was good enough that I decided to participate again the next year, and actually *try* to win.

And win, I did. As I've already detailed, my first experience winning National Novel Writing Month was by no means graceful or well-planned out, however, I learned quite a bit from my previous years participating. I knew more about my drafting habits and was starting my Bachelor's in Creative Writing, so to a point, I better understood the work ahead of me. But I think the thing that pulled me across the finish line in the end was the accountability. Here is what worked for me:

1. I found I got a buzz from updating my word count in the site tracker.
2. I told several people I was going to write a novel in a month.
3. Because most of those people were skeptical I could do it, I was going to prove them wrong.

I know that last point is a personality thing, but I can't argue with the results. I *won* that year, and those lessons have educated my approach to NaNo-WriMo ever since.

While accountability is a key to growth and success during NaNoWriMo, sometimes it's a journey to find a rewards system that motivates you. In my opinion, the best way to find something that works is to research multiple strategies or ideas and start trying stuff out. Don't be afraid to abandon systems that aren't working. If it is too stressful, too complicated or has too many moving parts, you may need to evaluate and simplify your process. These rewards systems should push you, not paralyze you.

You may also find that systems that have worked in the past will become inexplicably ineffective. This is a tough obstacle to overcome, so I have to have multiple failsafe strategies in case one of my go-tos stops working.

My three favorite strategies are keeping track of my word count in my calendar, a sticker or rewards chart, and verbal accountability with a writing buddy. As I go into detail, keep in mind that the possibilities for other methods are endless—be thinking of additional ways you can hold yourself responsible for your work.

STRATEGY #1: KEEP TRACK OF YOUR WORD COUNT IN YOUR CALENDAR

Out of all the strategies I use, this one is the most useful to me because it provides the data I need to adjust my process over the course of November. This will be important later.

After I complete a session, I record the number of words I wrote in the title of the appointment. I do this because it allows me to see how well I did in a session, especially if I over-achieve. If I manage to exceed the word count in my session, I get a huge boost of motivation to see how many *more* words I can write. The trick to this is I **do not** adjust my word count targets in response, so the extra words I write compound day over day.

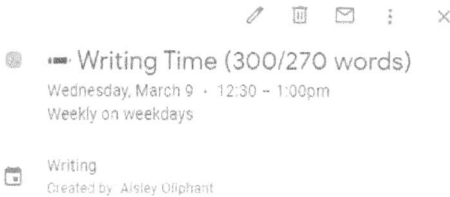

An example of tracking word count in a calendar appointment.

In the case I fall short of my goal, I can see exactly how many words I'll need to write to recover ground. I've found scheduling a smaller session later or trying to close the gap by over-shooting my target the next time I write helps in this situation, but I'll go into this more in Chapter 3.

STRATEGY #2: STICKER OR REWARDS CHART

I can be very externally motivated. For NaNoWriMo 2020, I rewarded myself with colored, foil star stickers each time I wrote a set number of words. The more words I wrote, the bigger the star sticker was and the more I got. This worked well because it gave me a blast of dopamine to see all my hard work laid out on the page.

But this is not the only way to construct an awards system. A handful of authors I have watched on YouTube like to set rewards like new phones, a trip to the bookstore, or dinner at a nice restaurant for some of the larger word count milestones. If you prefer to focus on days written or sessions completed, you can come up with a rewards system based on that.

This strategy has a lot of room for creativity, so don't be afraid to try new things or search for different ideas. I recommend talking to other writer friends to see how they self-motivate, or Google searching the motivational tools of people you look up to, and giving everything that sounds interesting to you a try.

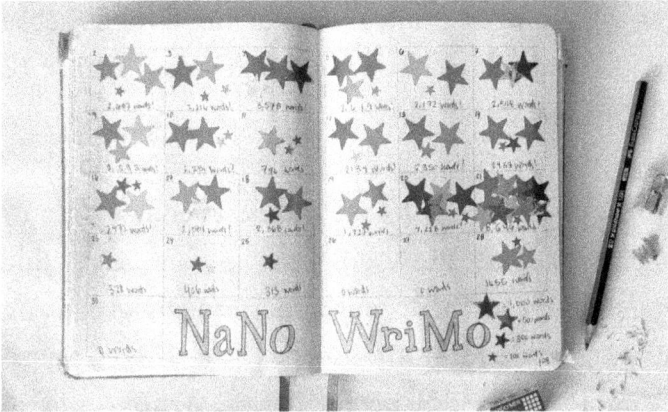

My motivational star sticker chart from NaNoWriMo 2020.
Photo by Jessica Sedgwick.

STRATEGY #3: ACCOUNTABILITY WITH WRITING BUDDIES

If you find it easier to stick to goals when you talk to someone, this strategy will work for you.

Being accountable to a writing buddy or buddies during National Novel Writing Month creates a support system and a sense of community. It lets you know there are others who are doing the same things as you or are going through similar struggles. I've found amazing support and encouragement when I've reported a bad writing day and celebrated the good. Writing friends also tend to be within reach whenever you need them. I have gone through stretches where I've texted friends weekly, and I've done daily word count accountability through social media, but you can set up any kind of cadence or system you would like!

But what if you don't have any writing buddies? You can reach out to supportive friends or family members instead. Additionally, you can find community online through social media groups or, as of the writing of this book, the "My Groups" feature on the National Novel Writing Month website. If you're using social media, try researching for groups or hashtags for groups that like to write the same genres as you or looking for NaNoWriMo support groups. While searching on the NaNoWriMo website, you could look for writing groups in your area or support writers of a specific genre. No matter where you choose to look, the point of having accountability buddies is to help you when things are hard, celebrate with you when things are good, and cheer you along when you've fallen behind.

CHAPTER 3
CATCH-UP STRATEGIES

"You just can't beat the person who never gives up."
—Babe Ruth, *The Rotarian*, July 1940[1]

C atching up is the most painful part of National Novel Writing Month for me. For years, I did it by isolating myself for an entire weekend or staying up until the wee hours of the morning 'till I wrote nonsense in my sleep. I said "no" to all opportunities and socially "went dark." I tried a lot of things that work when you don't have much on your plate outside a job and a small handful of responsibilities. But not everybody has that luxury. I lost it as I got older and more independent.

I'm not going to lie to you: falling behind in

National Novel Writing Month is inevitable. Even during the years that I've performed the best, I had days where I fell below the needed word count. Life will interfere and there is nothing we can do except adapt. It is critical to have a plan or strategies in place to help you catch back up, otherwise it is too easy to give up on pursuing your goal of finishing 50,000 words by the end of November.

To help me surmount the overwhelm and hopelessness that come from heavy catch-up work and too little time, I use four strategies to quickly get back on track: writing ahead, redistributing word count, writing in the cracks, and scheduling a write-in with friends. These four strategies produce amazing results for me, however, please feel free to come up with or search for ideas on your own that will work best with your writing process.

STRATEGY #1: WRITE AHEAD

My favorite strategy is to "write ahead" in every drafting session. This means I put extra effort into squeezing out as many words *over* my scheduled count as I can. How many words I write is entirely dependent on how much time I have left when I hit word count, but I always try to get a little more, even if it is just two or three words.

Using this strategy produces a useful buffer against bad days. If for some reason you can't hit a session's word count, or if you need to take a sick day, this padding of extra words can be a godsend. Consider, for example, if out of 100 writing sessions, you wrote ten words *over* your target word count. That's at least 1,000 extra words! In the scope of National Novel Writing Month, that is 600 words away from the site's recommended daily word count.

STRATEGY #2: REDISTRIBUTING WORD COUNT

Redistributing your remaining word count is a great strategy for getting back on track after a string of less-than-ideal writing sessions. The purpose is to minimize stress by spreading the catch-up weight across all your remaining days. It is miserable trying to recover ground all at once, and if you can lessen collateral damage to your mental health by increasing your load by just a few more words per session, your future self will thank you.

To calculate your redistribution, first look at

your calendar and figure out how much writing time you allocated for the rest of the month. Then, grab the number of words you have left to write before the end of the month and slide them into the following equations to figure out how many words per minute you will need to write to finish in time.

$$50{,}000 \text{ words} - X \text{ words written} = Y \text{ words remaining}$$

$$Y \text{ words remaining} \div Z \text{ hours left} = A \text{ words per hour (wph)}$$

$$A \text{ wph} \div 60 \text{ minutes} = B \text{ words per minute (wpm)}$$

Let's say you are on day 20 of NaNoWriMo, 10,000 words behind (that is to say, you have written 23,340 words), and you have 20 hours of writing time left in the month. The equations would look like this:

$$50{,}000 \text{ words} - 23{,}340 \text{ words written} = 26{,}660 \text{ words remaining}$$

$$26{,}660 \text{ words remaining} \div 20 \text{ hours left} = 1{,}333 \text{ wph}$$

$$1{,}333 \text{ wph} \div 60 \text{ minutes} = \text{approx. } 23 \text{ wpm}$$

Once you have your words per minute, go through the writing appointments you set in your calendar and recalculate how many words you will need to write each session as shown in Step 3 of "Use Time Blocking to Plan Your Month" on page 9. To continue with our previous example:

30-minute writing session × 23 wpm = 690 words

While your new target to write 690 words in one 30-minute session on its own can sound like a tall order, in the grand scheme of things, it is a lot easier to accomplish than trying to catch up all 10,000 of your words in a night. Just be sure writing 23 wpm is a feasible speed for you, but we'll get further into that in Chapter 4.

STRATEGY #3: WRITING IN THE CRACKS

Before I began working from home, I commuted about an hour and a half both ways, waiting for both the train and a tram to get to my day job. To take full advantage of my wait time, I made my manuscript available on my phone through Google Docs and wrote as much as I could before my transit arrived. I also took the time to write while I waited in line for lunch, or any other moment I had a break. To ensure I could track word count, I'd write in another font or in bold and record my total later.

This is exactly how "writing in the cracks" works: you find cracks of time in your day and cram in as many words as you can. This strategy is great for people who spend a lot of time waiting in lines, for public transportation, or anyone else who can snag five minutes here or ten minutes there.

For those who do not spend much time waiting around or commuting, writing in the cracks could also look like sneaking in a handful of words as the kids are sleeping or those last quiet moments right before bed. Maybe you've got a few minutes while waiting for dinner to cook, your kids to get out of school, your car to get fixed, or at your doctor's appointment. Wherever those brief moments of scrap time show up, take full advantage of them by writing what you can.

There are also multiple ways you can make your manuscript available to you anywhere. If Google Drive doesn't work for you, find another cloud service that does. You could even carry around a notebook to draft in when you find those stolen moments. Get a tool that fits your process and run with it, keeping in mind that whatever you choose needs to lend itself to helping you get ahead on your word count. Once you have your system in place, you will be surprised to see how quickly those fistfuls of words will add up and help you recover or maintain your ground over the month.

STRATEGY #4: SCHEDULE A WRITE-IN WITH FRIENDS

Friends can be a huge motivator when the going gets tough. If you find yourself losing motivation or feeling hopeless with the amount of work you need to do to catch up, coordinating a write-in could be just the thing to restart your engine.

Organizing time for you to write with others, or "write-in," can take any form you are comfortable with: video, chat room, in person, etc. You can also structure it any way you like! I know many writers that conduct twenty-minute drafting sprints with five to ten-minute rests in between to talk about everyone's progress. However you decide you want to work it, make sure the structure helps you get words written, rather than distract you.

If scheduling a write-in sounds overwhelming and too stressful, you can always join a write-in run by other writers through YouTube. These write-ins happen all the time and can offer just as much camaraderie and motivation as getting your own group together.

All of these catch-up strategies are powerful tools with the ability to help you make up a ton of work when you need it. But what if you have been using these strategies and can't seem to make headway?

CHAPTER 4

REALISTIC EXPECTATIONS, GOALS, AND BOUNDARIES

"If you align expectations with reality, you will never
be disappointed."
—Terrell Owens[1]

I became painfully aware of how I allowed National Novel Writing Month to affect my life a few weeks after I got married.

We were visiting my family on a weekend when I expressed to them I was finally participating in NaNoWriMo after taking a forced two-year break. I was excited, until my mom broke in and said, "Oh, you mean No-Fun November?" She then laughed and looked my new husband dead in the eye.

"She's your problem now."

Oof. Talk about a wake-up call.

Looking back at the NaNoWriMos that led up to this moment, I can't in good faith say I was a pleasant person. The mounting stress of trying to finish a book in thirty days caused me to lash out and be cranky most of the month, but I was so focused on "doing the thing" that I wasn't aware of how my poor handling of stress affected those around me. Digging deeper, I realized there was more iceberg to this problem than I knew.

Compounded with the stress of hitting daily word counts were the unrealistic expectations and goals I had set for myself. I had no boundaries, didn't make time to nurture relationships or allow myself any rest, and I expected myself to write 2,000 words per day, six days a week, all while balancing work and school. While I loved it, it was misery, and it made my family miserable too.

Reaching your goals should be a fun, exciting adventure that leads you to self-fulfillment, not a soul-sucking endeavor that becomes a self-imposed whipping post. It shouldn't drop a nuke on your relationships, either. There will likely come a point in this journey where you have to stop and examine your goals, expectations, and boundaries so they align with what you physically, mentally, and emotionally can do. This will minimize the stress of completing such a Herculean feat as writing a book in a month and decrease collateral damage.

Let's take a closer look about what it means to set realistic expectations, goals, and boundaries that support your writing, your well-being, *and* your life.

SETTING REALISTIC EXPECTATIONS

Setting realistic expectations for yourself gets sticky and complicated because there are so many factors that make up our capacity to get things done. A good handful of those things are non-negotiable, like paying bills, nutrition, sleep, family time, medical needs, etc. Life has a way of prioritizing itself with all types of emergencies and problems we must take care of.

Some important reminders:

Be flexible when people *really* need you. You may have set expectations and boundaries with your loved ones about your writing time, but make sure you are carving out time for the people who mean the most in your life. Not everything is an emergency, but do your best to be in tune to those key moments when you need to be present for someone you love.

Cut yourself slack if you can't meet your word

count every writing session. It really isn't the end of the world, even though I know sometimes it feels that way. Beating yourself up over falling short is an easy trap to fall into. Instead, look at it as an opportunity to adjust your sails and keep writing.

It's okay to take a rest day if you need it! One of my favorite quotes on this concept comes from David Horsager's *The Trust Edge*: "You don't have to be productive 100% of the time; just choose your downtime so your downtime doesn't choose you" (209)[2]. This means that unless you give yourself time to rest, your body will *force* you to rest. Sickness, burnout, breakdown, and more can take you out for extended periods and put you behind. Taking a day of rest now and again will help you be more effective at the keyboard because it allows you to recover energy and motivation. Attempting to work through burnout or sickness only worsens the problem, making it hard for you to get back in the saddle later.

Make sure your capacity and skills match your expected output. To illustrate what matching skills and capacity to outcome looks like, let's say when you sit down to redistribute your word count, you realize in order to finish National Novel Writing Month in time, you will need to write 90 wpm in your remaining writing sessions. Realistically, not many people can type that fast (the average adult can type about 40 wpm[3]), and this speed does not necessarily factor in the time your brain will stop and think about what you are writing. This is a prime example of when you may need to adjust your expectations and goals to match what you can actually do.

It is best to discover snags like this before you start working; however, if you're like me, you may need to re-evaluate your expectations often. I don't tend to know what is realistic for me until I've crashed and burned over too-ambitious goals multiple times.

In addition, it may be pertinent to do a self-check and make sure you aren't hamstringing yourself by wasting too much time. Take a critical look at how much time you spend procrastinating by watching extra TV or scrolling. Remember, a little wasted time is okay (choose your downtime), but a lot can prevent you from getting done what needs doing.

SETTING REALISTIC GOALS

There is no shame in adjusting your goals so you can reach them.

I'm going to say that one more time.

There is no shame in adjusting your goals so you can reach them!

Now, I'm not saying sterilize your goals so they are too easy to reach. I'm saying lower the bar just enough that you can reach it, but you still have to stretch to get it.

I'll give you an example.

After I finished my first manuscript, I was chomping at the bit to get it to beta readers. I had vague ideas of things that needed changing, but I was clueless where to start my big-picture edits. Rather than giving myself ample time to do a thorough self-edit (as I should have), I set the goal to do a month-long editing blitz, then blast out the manuscript to betas for feedback.

Spoiler: this was not a realistic goal.

What I thought would be a quick copyediting pass turned into the aforementioned thorough self-edit. My beta reader deadline crept closer and closer, and I was nowhere near finishing. For me, this deadline was non-negotiable because it involved keeping promises to others, so instead of quitting or being late, I stepped back and evaluated what I *could* do.

What I *could* do was drop what chapters I had to betas a chunk at a time and continue my self-edits. I changed my goal to sending my betas three chapters per week, starting on the promised deadline, and self-editing another three chapters per week to match the release schedule. This new goal was still challenging and fulfilled my commitments, but broke the work down into a more manageable timeline.

You also can do something similar while participating in National Novel Writing Month. Yes, the general goal and point of National Novel Writing Month is to write 50,000 words; however, it isn't illegal to adapt the word count to what you can do. There is even a place on the official NaNoWriMo website where you can adjust the word count goal you are shooting for and calculate the milestones for you!

Here are three steps you can take to determine what might be a more realistic goal for you to reach if 50,000 words isn't plausible at the moment.

STEP 1: TAKE STOCK OF WHAT YOU CAN DO

To begin, ask yourself, what is my limiting factor?

Limiting factors can come in as many shapes and sizes as there are people. I could wax long on how each of them could be handled, but I would not be able to cover them all and it would take too long. For the sake of brevity, here are ideas on how you can overcome two of the most common limiting factors, typing speed and time remaining.

Typing Speed

If you feel like the typing speed you need to maintain to finish in time is unsustainable, determine what a realistic wpm would look like for you instead. Not sure what is a good speed for you? Take a quick typing test online to find out. Then multiply your wpm by how many hours you have left times sixty minutes to find a more realistic word count goal.

X wpm × Y hours remaining × 60 minutes = Z words by the end of the month

Once you know how many words you could get by the end of the month at that typing speed, add it to your running total to determine your new word count goal. Let's take a look at another example.

In our equations from "Redistributing Word Count" on page 27, we determined that if we are

10,000 words behind on NaNoWriMo day twenty, we would need to write approximately twenty-three words per minute to finish in twenty hours. But say you don't feel it's feasible for you to write twenty-three words per minute, but you know you could pull off typing nine words per minute to factor in thinking time.

$$9 \text{ wpm} \times 20 \text{ hours remaining} \times 60 \text{ minutes} = 10,800 \\ \text{words by the end of month}$$

Add that total to how many words you've already written and you could feasibly reset your goal to 34,140 words by November 30th!

$$10,800 + 23,340 \text{ words written} = 34,140 \text{ words by end} \\ \text{of month}$$

But what if your ability to type quickly isn't the problem? What if it is an unexpected decrease in time?

Time Remaining

As I've said many times before, life has a way of throwing curveballs at the expense of your free time.

If you find yourself with less time than you anticipated, revisit your calendar and make your best guess on how much of your schedule your new obligations will take up. In this process, some of your writing sessions may need to be sacrificed, but whenever you can, try to reschedule them (though this may not be possible in every case).

After your schedule is rearranged, recalculate your remaining writing time. Then use your previously calculated words per minute to figure out how many words you can hit with your time remaining:

$$X \text{ wpm} \times Y \text{ hours remaining} \times 60 \text{ minutes} = Z \text{ words by end of month}$$

Add that to the number of words you've already written to get a more realistic idea of what you can accomplish with the remaining time you have.

To borrow from our previous example, if you've already written 23,340 words, have only ten hours left to write, and can type comfortably at 9 wpm, you would be able to write 5,400 more words before NaNoWriMo ends.

$$9 \text{ wpm} \times 10 \text{ hours remaining} \times 60 \text{ minutes} = 5,400 \text{ words by end of month}$$

Add 5,400 to the words you've already written, and you could feasibly write a total of 28,740 words come November 30th.

23,340 words written + 5,400 words to write = 28,740 words by end of month

STEP 2: TIME BLOCK IT ALL OUT

Now that your writing plan has changed, your calendar needs to reflect those changes. Just like in Chapter 1, go through and make sure you have time blocked for your writing sessions, as well as whatever new obligations have come up. If you don't know how long something is going to take, make your best guess and adjust your schedule later. Commit to keeping those remaining writing appointments and make sure you know what each session's target word count is.

STEP 3: SET UP ACCOUNTABILITY

It can be discouraging to have to change your goals, but remember: progress is progress, no matter what it looks like. To help you keep your eye on the prize and continue pushing toward your new goals, set up accountability systems to help you see how well you are doing.

Again, this will look different for everyone, so make sure you pick a system that works well for you and lifts you up. Revisiting your sticker charts, reaching out to friends, adjusting your goals on the National Novel Writing Month website, and tracking word count in your calendar are all viable ways to help you see how far you've come.

SETTING REALISTIC BOUNDARIES

Boundaries are important because they help you make good on the time you've set aside for yourself and your writing. Without them, your "flow state," or the intense cognitive state where you are completely immersed in an activity[4], will break and your writing productivity and creativity will suffer.

While planning out how we are going to win National Novel Writing Month, we must set multiple boundaries to find success. Three of the biggest areas that need them are with our relationships, technology, and ourselves. If you can set clear and manageable boundaries in these three areas, your chances of reaching 50,000 words by November 30th will drastically increase.

Relationships

Boundaries in relationships are hard to balance because it is generally impossible for us to just shut ourselves away for long stretches at a time to get writing done. Most everyone has obligations to family, friends, co-workers, and others that they cannot ignore. The best thing you can do for yourself and others during National Novel Writing Month is make sure you have clear communication with everyone whose relationship will be impacted by your absence during writing time.

The best time to communicate your boundaries with your friends, family, roommates, kids, et cetera is when you've established your game plan. Let them know when you are writing, where you will be writing (if necessary), and under what circumstances you can be interrupted. If it's helpful, post a sign on the door to the room you'll be working in to remind those around you to DO NOT DISTURB. Help these people understand you're serious by enforcing those boundaries whenever they are broken, and don't be discouraged if it takes multiple infractions before they understand.

Because these boundary-breakers are probably just looking to spend time with you, *make a special effort to block time for them on the calendar.* This will look different for every person. Personally, I block Sunday evenings for family dinners/game nights and a couple hours a week for date night with my husband. I also make sure I'm not working on holidays like Thanksgiving so I can visit extended family members. Maybe you're watching a specific TV show with your roommates, or you need to set aside an hour to play with kids or pets. Planning this time is critical. Your relationships and mental health shouldn't become collateral damage in your conquest to finish a novel in a month.

Another good way to help you manage your boundaries with your loved ones and others you associate with is to let them in on what you are doing. Update them on your progress and allow them to share your excitement for your story. My favorite thing to do with my husband is to talk through sticky points in my manuscript. Bouncing ideas off him in the moments when I'm mired deep in a plot hole or writer's block is refreshing, and he is encouraging when I experience self-doubt or discouragement. Including those you care about in your process will likely increase your support and give them motivation to respect the boundaries you've set.

Technology

Managing boundaries around technology can be challenging because it involves the one person who is bound to distract you the most... yourself. Everyone's use of technology looks different, however it's universal enough that it can do incredible damage to your motivation, creativity, and productivity during National Novel Writing Month. It's difficult to ignore the consistent shoulder-tap of emails, updates, texts, calls, comments, likes, and the desire to do "research" for your story, especially if you are resisting the work.

The first step in setting boundaries around technology is acknowledging what is most difficult for you to resist. Do you feel the need to respond to every social media comment immediately? Do you get lost scrolling through memes? Are you addicted to negative political commentaries and hot takes on YouTube? Or do you have a tendency to fall into rabbit holes after looking up a small piece of information to help perfect your world building? Make a list of all the things about technology that distract you.

Next, study your list and think about ways you can set boundaries around your technology use that will protect you from these distractions. Feel free to get creative in this. You could write without the internet and take notes of things to research. Give your phone to a family member for safekeeping until your writing time is over. You could log out of or delete social media apps on your phone to give you an extra barrier of entry. Or maybe technological distractions are too much altogether, and you need to write in a quiet room with just a notebook and pen. How you decide to insulate yourself from technological distractions is up to you. Just make sure your chosen methods work. There is no sense in writing with your phone across the room if all you're going to do is think about what you're missing while you work.

Self

Even though you can be your greatest distractor, you are also your greatest asset. Setting boundaries with yourself is one of the healthiest things you can do for yourself during this month of late nights, early mornings, and long writing sessions. It's easy to get caught up in the excitement of the challenge, push yourself to your limits, and to see what you can accomplish. This is exhilarating; however it is unsustainable for long periods of time and may damage your mental and physical health.

Be sure to set boundaries with yourself as you embark on this great journey. Block time in your schedule to rest and rejuvenate, and do your best to make that time non-negotiable. During that relaxation block, do things that make you feel happy, more like yourself, and bring you joy. Giving yourself quality time will increase your productivity in the long run and help you tackle the challenge of writing 50,000 words in a way that pushing yourself to your breaking point can't. As I've mentioned before, I do this by taking the day off on Sundays to rest and rejuvenate. While this might not be the answer for everyone because it increases the necessary daily word count to win, blocking a few hours a day for self-care can be just as effective.

The next thing you can do is remember that National Novel Writing Month isn't a game about quality, it is about *quantity*. You can't expect every word to pour forth from your fingers to be perfect, poetic, and well-crafted. Holding yourself to a Shakespearean-level of prose is going to slow you down and frustrate you. Write what comes to you and know that you can fix it later. One of my favorite quotes from Neil Gaiman says, "In a first draft, you get to explode. The objective (at least for me) is to get it down on paper, somehow. Battle through the laziness and the not-enough-time and the this-is-rubbish and everything else, and just get it written. Whatever it takes. The second draft is where you go and gather together the fragments of the explosion and figure out what it is you did, and make it look like that was what you always meant to do."[5] Letting go of perfectionism with the under-standing you can go back and revise will help you reach the word count bars you've set and ultimately relieve the mental pressure of producing a perfect product on the first try.

Finally, learn to recognize when you are burning out or feeling stretched too thin, and take a break. Do you feel like you're metaphorically "going to die?" Are you unable to face your workstation another day or you'll go crazy? Give yourself permission to stop. You can catch up later. It's not the end of the world if you can't hit your word count every session, and you are going to have bad days. It is much better to plan in time for setbacks and rest than it is to destroy your mental health over an annual challenge.

If you feel like conducting a self-check is difficult for you, or you are unsure of what the symptoms of burnout, unrealistic goals or boundaries could look like, visit the self-assessment section on page 69 for quizzes. While these are **not** a substitute for professional medical advisement, they are designed to help you decide if you need to take a step back, reevaluate, or ask for help.

CHAPTER 5
MAKING THE MOST OF YOUR DRAFTING TIME

"[Your manuscript] doesn't have to be perfect. It doesn't have to be good. It just has to exist so you can make it better."

—V. E. Schwab, NaNoWriMo Pep Talk, 2019[1]

Discovering the best way to make the most of your time is challenging, involving everything from psychological conditioning to ritual creation. You need to be able to hit the keyboard typing and ready to go, with little to no pauses between words. But once you find your sweet spot or process, you'll start to reap big rewards.

While working onsite at my full-time job, I found I was most productive during my lunch-hour writing sessions when I went to the same place every day at the same time, popped in headphones with instrumental music, and set myself a timer to compete against. The mantra of my afternoon became, "I only have thirty minutes to get this done," and I worked as fast as I could before going back to work.

This functioned like a dream for me. Most days, I could get in the flow right away and exceed my word count goals by 100 or 200 words. I'd walk into the room and I instantly feel the drive to write. There were some days when others managed to claim my secret hideaway room before I could get there, but listening to a specific type of music as I wrote made the transition to a new, temporary space manageable and productive.

It can take a lot of trial and error to figure out a routine that works for you (it took days of wandering to find a room in my office building deserted enough for me), so I've got a handful of ideas you can begin testing for yourself. My list is by no means exhaustive; use these as a jumping-off point as you experiment with strategies that help you get the most out of your writing.

STRATEGY #1: RETYPE THE LAST PARAGRAPH OR LINE YOU WROTE

In his book *Million Dollar Productivity*, Kevin J. Anderson suggests that the act of rewriting your last page, sentence, or paragraph can help "get your mind in gear" or launch you into the mindset of writing. It helps you remember what you wrote last and be able to pick up where you left off (Anderson, 41-42)[2].

When I do this, I generally retype the last paragraph at the most, as it doesn't take nearly as much time as retyping entire pages. The mechanical motion greases my creative gears, making it so much easier for me to remember where I was going with a scene or a snatch of dialogue. That forward momentum propels me the rest of the way through my session and allows me to reach my word count goals more efficiently.

If you decide to try this, be mindful of your time constraints and only retype a length of text that will leave you with sufficient time and energy to write new words that will count toward your goal. A little can go a long way in this instance, but don't be afraid to work with larger chunks of text, if that is what your process demands.

STRATEGY #2: SET THE MOOD

Setting the mood is arranging a string of stimuli or habits that put your mind into drive when it's time to write. The science behind this follows the results of Pavlov's dog experiment. Simplified, Pavolv would ring a bell, then he would feed the dogs. He did this multiple times, causing the dogs to become conditioned to salivate any time they heard the bell ring.[3] When I would abscond to my hidden office space to draft, the smell of the 1970's upholstered couches next to the desk became the stimulus that helped my brain know it was time to write.

For you, this could look like making yourself a particular drink when it's time to write, writing in the same place, or turning on a specific type of music. You could choose a particular scent of candle, essential oils, or sound to condition yourself to be ready to write. If it's helpful, you could also create rituals out of any combination of these things to get you into the mood to work. Once you've decided which stimuli you would like to use, only use those scents, smells, habits, sounds, locations, etc. when you are getting ready to write, otherwise their triggering effect won't be as potent.

STRATEGY #3: ENGAGE WITH YOUR BELIEF SYSTEM

Where do you believe your muse or your ideas come from? Belief systems and muses are incredibly diverse and powerful.

Personally, I like to pray before writing sessions and ask God for help solving plot problems and getting ideas. Sarra Cannon, author of the Shadow Demons Saga and other witchy fantasy books, reads tarot cards, journals, and sets out her favorite crystals to energize her before sitting down to write[4]. Brandon Sanderson, bestselling fantasy author of the Stormlight Archives, will take time to read scriptures before he begins work[5], and Kevin J. Anderson, New York Times bestselling co-author of *Dune: House Atreides*, will activate his muse on long hikes in the mountains (Anderson, 22)[6].

Whatever belief system you ascribe to, take the time to do research or soul-search to learn what you can do to call upon that power and use it to help you make the most of the time you set aside for writing.

STRATEGY #4: BRAINSTORM IN THE CRACKS

Earlier in this book, you'll remember I mentioned writing in the cracks of your day, such as when you're waiting to commute or standing in line. But what if you don't have the ability to draft in those moments?

In *Million Dollar Productivity*, Kevin J. Anderson states:

> "If you find yourself in a place where you really can't jot down detailed notes (say, in the gym or waiting in line at the grocery store), use every little snatch of time to ponder *what* you're going to write the next time you get a few minutes at your keyboard. Do your mulling ahead of time, so that when you do have a few spare moments to sit with your butt in the chair and your fingers to the keys, you can jump right in and get down to actual writing instead of pondering what you mean to say" (51).

I love this strategy because it's easy to freeze up if you know you are racing against time. Your typing speed slows the more you have to consider what you're saying or where you're going. By having thought through the scenes you are going to write, your brain is well lubricated and more likely to keep up with the speed you need to type to stay on track.

STRATEGY #5: REVIEW YOUR NOTES THE NIGHT BEFORE

For those who thrive off of outlining (also known as *"planners"*), reading your notes and outlines the night before can be a huge boost in creativity. If you prefer discovery writing, or writing without an outline (*"pantsing"*), making a quick plan or taking the time to imagine what parts you'll write before bed can have the same effect. I am a discovery writer learning how to outline (a *plantser*, if you will), so I'll usually read over or write out a handful of the bullet points summarizing scenes or beats I will be covering the next day. The times that I have done this, I have woken up realizing my brain worked it in the background and made my subsequent writing sessions much easier to push through.

STRATEGY #6: CREATE A MOOD OR INSPIRATION BOARD FOR YOUR PROJECT

A mood or inspiration board for your work-in-progress is a great trigger to get the creative juices flowing. Images have a strong effect on the brain, and chances are when you picked specific images to represent your story, there was something about them that was compelling or exciting.

I love doing this, as it helps me remember how much I love the images that seeded my idea. Pinterest is my go-to method for creating mood and inspiration boards, but there are many other ways you can make them. I've seen writers on Instagram and YouTube create physical collages for their offices or compile collections using sites like Unsplash.com. Whatever method you choose, quickly reviewing these images before writing can help renew that sense of motivation, wonder, and excitement for the project, thereby giving you a wave to ride as you push toward your word count goals.

CHAPTER 6
DEALING WITH FAILURE

"It is possible to commit no mistakes and still lose.
That is not a weakness. That is life." ·
—Jean-Luc Picard[1]

S ometimes life and its emergencies win. And you know what? That is okay. It happens. Maybe you get close to finishing NaNoWriMo and miss by a hair. Maybe you miss by a longshot. Whatever your case is, know that failures aren't permanent and serve as a great way to help you learn and grow.

Each time I lost National Novel Writing Month, it taught me something key about my process that didn't work. I learned that finding time to write worked better when I put it in my schedule instead of doing it when I found myself twiddling my thumbs. I learned blindly writing as many words as I could in a session didn't motivate me because the word count milestones weren't bite sized or trackable enough. I learned I get more done when I focus on writing in smaller spurts, rather than holding out for large chunks of time.

I'm not saying that it never hurts when I lose NaNoWriMo. It hurts a lot—especially when I've given it 110%. But it doesn't have to be something that ruins your life when it happens.

Here are a few things to remember when working through and dealing with failure.

It is okay to feel your feelings. Take time to process the emotions that come with failing to reach your goals. Are you angry or disappointed? Do you feel sad? Allow yourself a little space to mourn or feel bad and then let it go. Don't let yourself ruminate or stew for too long, otherwise it will be difficult to pull yourself out and try again.

You are not defined by your failures. If you miss that deadline or undershoot your NaNoWriMo goals, it is not a commentary on who you are as a person. It's not even a commentary on the challenge or deadline. Don't allow yourself to get sucked into the notion that the challenge set before you was bad, or that failure is suddenly an intrinsic part of your nature.

Look for the lessons you learned. Something can always be learned from a failure. Take a moment to look back and see what you could do better. What worked well for you? What didn't? Chances are you know more about your creative process than you did when you started. Decide to take those learnings forward for next time.

Acknowledge your successes, no matter how small. A friend once told me that if I had the right attitude, I'd never have a bad day, just a hard day. Amidst those hard days is *always* a smattering of good. Make a list of all the "wins" you had over the course of the month, regardless of size. This could be something like making the time to write on a day where the entire universe seemed against you. It could be filling in that plot hole that stalked you like a panther all month. Tip your hat to the work you managed to do and how far you got. At the end of it all, you have more of a book written than you did when you started!

You can always try again. Not every failure is final. Thirty-day challenges like National Novel Writing Month tend to occur yearly, and you can give finishing a book in a month another crack! New and fresh opportunities will always come around, whether it be Camp NaNoWriMo or making time to write in the "off" season. You're *not required* to finish your book during NaNoWriMo. No matter what your case is, you'll get another shot.

CHAPTER 7
FINAL THOUGHTS

"Don't think, *Can I?* Instead think, *How can I?* Then start moving forward. The moment you confront *and act* on a problem, you begin to solve it."
—John Maxwell, Developing the Leader Within You 2.0[1]

Writing a novel in a month is a beast when your schedule doesn't have much wiggle room. But just because your calendar is tight, doesn't mean you can't reach your goals or shouldn't try. Blocking out your calendar, setting up accountability, having catch-up strategies ready, and evaluating your expectations, goals, and boundaries regularly are incredibly influential tools that can help you amp up your NaNoWriMo game. They allow you to find and prioritize pockets of time for your writing, and for people like myself who frequently find themselves booked to the gills, every second counts.

Don't forget everyone's journey is different. I developed this strategy over years of trial and error, and it ultimately enabled me to finish writing 50,000 words easily within eighteen days. Your path could look exactly the same as mine and all my ideas could work for you. Or, it's possible only *some* or even *none* of the things I shared work for you and you'll need to find a way to fill in your personal gaps. But the growth I experienced while developing this strategy feels incredible and it is something that is accessible to you, too. The skills in this book can assist anyone towards success, even if it is as simple as providing an idea of how you can work better with your brain and writing process.

Take the time to stretch yourself and hone your writing practice. In *Developing the Leader Within You 2.0*, John Maxwell says, "Ideas evolve as you move, and better solutions come into view as you move forward" (Maxwell, 114). The more you participate in these types of challenges, the better, more streamlined your process will get. You will start to feel yourself improve. You will eventually succeed. All you need to do is jump in, stay creative, and be unafraid to make mistakes.

Now get out there and plan yourself a win!

SELF-ASSESSMENT
QUESTIONNAIRES

HOW DO I KNOW IF I'M BURNING OUT?

Burnout is destructive and can put you out of commission long-term. In order to win thirty-day writing challenges, managing burnout is critical. Use the questionnaire below to determine whether you are beginning to feel the effects of burnout.

DISCLAIMER: THIS QUESTIONNAIRE IS NOT A SUBSTITUTE FOR PROFESSIONAL MEDICAL ADVICE. PLEASE CONSULT A MEDICAL PROFESSIONAL OR HEALTHCARE PROVIDER IF YOU ARE SEEKING MEDICAL ADVICE, DIAGNOSIS, OR TREATMENT.

1. Do you feel stressed when you think about your next writing session?

2. Think about why you started writing this idea. Do you feel exhausted, unmotivated, or doubtful?
3. Is every day a bad writing day?
4. Do you feel sick when you think about getting your words in for the day?
5. Do you feel your story will never work or that you can't work on it anymore?
6. Do you feel like you are stretched thin and no matter what you do, you can't keep up?
7. Do you feel dissatisfied or discouraged when you hit your target word count in a writing session?
8. Are you feeling physical symptoms of stress when you think about working on your thirty-day writing challenge?
9. Are you procrastinating your writing?
10. Are you getting frequent technology headaches from working?
11. Are you irritable all the time?
12. Are you lashing out at people?
13. Do you feel drained?
14. Do you find yourself overeating or undereating to cope with the stress?

If you answered "yes" to most of these questions,

consider taking time off of writing to relax. Make a plan to reach out to individuals in your life that can help you step away from your project until you are feeling better. Have compassion with yourself and accept that you will be more effective if you get some rest.

HOW DO I KNOW IF MY GOALS ARE REALISTIC?

Goals should motivate us and get us excited to write. They should never be used in self-flagellation or self-deprecation. They are intended to stimulate personal growth. Use these questions to determine if you have set realistic goals and whether or not you may need to reevaluate the bar you have set for yourself.

1. When you think about your goals, do you feel energized, confident, and empowered?
2. Do your goals motivate you to get out of bed and get to work?
3. Are your goals specific, measurable, attainable, rewarding, and trackable (SMART)[1]?

4. Can you realistically complete the work you need to do within the time frame you've given yourself?

5. Did you begin working on your goals feeling excited, but now have realized the work it will take to achieve it and feel stressed?

6. Do you feel you are able to give a consistent, dedicated effort to working on your goals?

7. Are you resisting the work you need to do for success by procrastination?

8. Are you prioritizing other commitments over your scheduled goal time?

9. Do you feel sick, stressed, or worried when you think about your goals?

If you answered "no" to questions 1-5, consider taking a step back and adjusting the parameters of your goals. There is no shame in adjusting your goals so you can reach them.

HOW DO I KNOW IF I'M SETTING REALISTIC EXPECTATIONS AND BOUNDARIES?

Setting realistic expectations is a key skill that can be developed. To begin determining if your expectations are realistic, use the following questions to evaluate your game plan.

1. Does the schedule I have set for myself include time for myself and others outside of writing?
2. Can I actually type as fast as I need to to hit my goal word count each session?
3. Does my target typing speed factor in pauses for thought?
4. Am I deleting more words in a session than I am writing?

5. Am I allowing myself to unleash during writing sessions and get in as many terrible words as I can?

6. Are the rules around my writing time too stringent for others to follow?

7. Am I willing to be flexible and make up the work another time when unexpected items come up?

8. Does the schedule I have set for myself allow me to take care of my physical needs such as sleep and meals?

9. Have I scheduled myself enough time to write the number of words I need to?

10. Do I feel like I am able to move around my schedule so I can take care of important or necessary unexpected items?

If you answered "no" to 8 out of 10 questions, consider taking a step back and reevaluating your expectations or boundaries.

Want physical copies of these questionaires?

Become an Insider today to access FREE *Booked to the Gills* self-assessment printables!

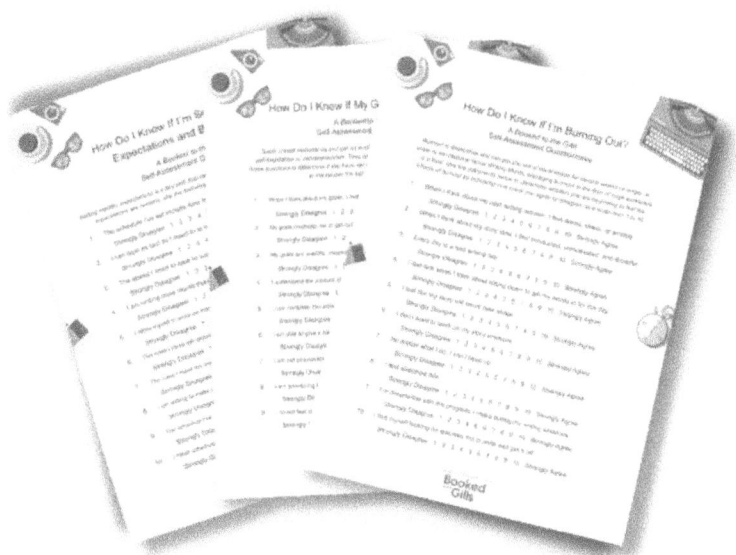

https://www.aisleyoliphant.com/insiderannex

NOTES

INTRODUCTION

1. Pianochick66. "NaNoWriMo - Poster V." *Deviant Art*, 6 Oct. 2009, www.deviantart.com/pianochick66/art/NaNoWriMo-Poster-V-139386940. Accessed 29 June 2022.
2. TED Talks. (2017). *How to gain control of your free time | Laura Vanderkam*. Retrieved December 1, 2021, from https://www.youtube.com/watch?v=n3kNlFMXs-lo&list=LL&index=175.

1. TIME BLOCKING

1. Penn, William. "The Preface." *The Harvard Classics: Fruits of Solitude*, vol. 1, P.F. COLLIER & SON, New York City, NY, 1909, www.bartleby.com/1/3/1004.html. Accessed 29 June 2022.

2. ACCOUNTABILITY

1. Pulsifer, Catherine. "Inspirational Quote Image." *Habits for Wellbeing*, HabitsforWellbeing.com, www.habitsforwellbeing.com/how-do-you-create-personal-accountability-in-your-life/at-the-end-of-the-day-we-are-accountable-to-ourselves-our-success-is-a-result-of-what-we-do-catherine-pulsifer/. Accessed 29 June 2022.
2. Johnson, S. (2020, July 22). *APPLYING PEARSON'S LAW TO RECRUITING AND RETENTION*. Rismedia. Retrieved

February 2, 2022, from shorturl.at/alqRV.

3. CATCH-UP STRATEGIES

1. Ruth, George Herman 'Babe.' "'Bat It Out!'" *The Rotarian*, July 1940, p. 14, ttps://books.google.com/books?id=IEEEAAAAMBAJ&q=%22never+gives%22&hl=en#v=snippet&q=%22never%20-gives%22&f=false.

4. REALISTIC EXPECTATIONS, GOALS, AND BOUNDARIES

1. Bensinger, Graham. "Terrell Owens Interview." *The Graham Bensinger Show*, ESPN, 5 Nov. 2005.
2. Horsager, David. *The Trust Edge: How Top Leaders Gain Faster Results, Deeper Relationships, and a Stronger Bottom Line.* Free Press, 2012.
3. *Typing Speed Infographic.* Ratatype.com - Learn to Type Faster. Retrieved January 4, 2022, from https://www.ratatype.com/learn/average-typing-speed/.
4. Psychology Today, S. (n.d.). *Flow.* Psychology Today. Retrieved February 4, 2022, from https://www.psychology-today.com/us/basics/flow
5. Gaiman, Neil. "YOU PUT YOUR (RIGHT-HAND REAR) LEG IN..." *Neil Gaiman's Journal*, 11 May 2008, journal.neil-gaiman.com/2008/05/you-put-your-right-hand-rear-leg-in.html.

5. MAKING THE MOST OF YOUR DRAFTING TIME

1. Schwab, V. E. "Pep Talk from V. E. Schwab." Received by National Novel Writing Month Participants, *NaNoWriMo*, National Novel Writing Month, 4 Nov. 2019, nanowrimo.org/pep-talk-from-v-e-schwab.
2. Anderson, Kevin J. *Million Dollar Productivity*. WordFire Press, 2014.
3. McLeod, Saul. "Pavlov's Dogs Study and Pavlovian Conditioning Explained." *Simply Psychology*, Simply Scholar Ltd, 2021, https://www.simplypsychology.org/pavlov.html.
4. Cannon, Sarra, director. *NaNoWriMo Diaries 2020. NaNoWriMo Diaries 2020 (Daily NaNoWriMo Vlogs)*, Heart Breathings, 2020, https://www.youtube.com/playlist?list=PLg6zjsQP4Pwf9ONFNNJ_qdZ_2cLYIzQo9. Accessed 2020.
5. Sanderson, B. (2021, January). Why I Believe with Brandon Sanderson. My Road to Hope and Peace. Facebook Live; Facebook Live.
6. Anderson, Kevin J. Million Dollar Productivity. WordFire Press, 2014.

6. DEALING WITH FAILURE

1. Kemper, David. "Star Trek: The Next Generation." Season 2, episode 21, 1989.

7. FINAL THOUGHTS

1. Maxwell, John C. *Developing the Leader Within You 2.0*. HarperCollins Leadership, 2018.

HOW DO I KNOW IF MY GOALS
ARE REALISTIC?

1. Mind Tools, C. T. (n.d.). *Personal Goal Setting: Planning to Live Your Life Your Way*. Mind Tools. Retrieved February 5, 2022, from https://www.mindtools.com/page6.html

Did you enjoy

Booked
to the Gills?

If so, please consider leaving a review on your favorite book retailer site!

Reviews are one of the easiest ways to support authors... aside from buying their books, of course!

ACKNOWLEDGMENTS

Good gracious, I have a lot of people to thank for helping me bring *Booked to the Gills* into your hands. I had a small, but incredible army of people encouraging me, pushing me, advising me, drying my tears... the whole kit and caboodle.

First off, I want to give a special thanks to Kevin J. Anderson, Allyson Longueira, and Mark Leslie Lefebvre for advising me on this project. Without their guidance, suggestions, and tutelage, this project would not exist in the form it does. I'm also grateful for the friends from my graduate program, as they also served as sounding boards and cheerleaders as I tried to circumvent the handful of manuscript problems I encountered these last few months.

I'd like to thank my wonderful legion of alpha and beta readers, Ben, Parker, Annabelle, Amelia, Jordan, Beth, Steph, Katie, Joni, Brian, Collin, Kyrsten, Elise, and Cody. Your feedback helped me beef this thing up from a free printable to a full-on book.

Thank you to my family, both on my husband's side and on mine, for their constant support. I can't tell you how much I appreciate you showing up for me, no matter what I do. Thanks as well to my friends, for offering me help, getting me out of the house for craft nights, dinner, or board games.

Very special thanks and award for the best spouse in the world goes to my sweet Jonah, for putting up with me and the intense workload I always pile on myself. He's my rock, my voice of reason, and I am so lucky to be the one that caught him.

And finally, I'd like to thank my production team, editors Courtney and Bob, who helped me polish this thing until it shone, Jessica, for being my IR, hype woman, and masterful photographer for this book, the MiblArt team for their absolutely fantastic cover art, and last but, but not least, both Kevin J. Anderson and Craig Martelle for providing me with amazing book blurbs. I appreciate their hard work in getting this book publication ready.

Putting this book in your hands has been an incredible, growth-promoting experience, and I wouldn't trade it for the world. Thank you to you, dear reader, for deciding to take a chance on me and giving *Booked to the Gills* a shot. You, my friend, are seriously the best.

Happy writing!

ABOUT THE AUTHOR

Aisley Oliphant has been in love with writing since she learned how to hold a pencil, creating wild stories about mermaids and far-fetched adventures with her friends. She received her Bachelor's degree in Creative Writing from Weber State University, became a writing tutor for the WSU Writing Center where she helped students one-on-one to self-edit and improve their writing. She went on to work as a writer and editorial assistant for *Utah Business Magazine,* and a freelance writer for her church, editing and publishing more than twenty-five articles in between them. In the summer of 2022, she graduated with a Masters of Publishing from Western Colorado University.

Currently, Aisley is preparing to start developmental edits on her debut fiction novel, and has also begun production on a graphic novel series. She was on the editorial staff for the *Gilded Glass: Twisted Myths & Shattered Fairy Tales* anthology by executive editors Kevin J. Anderson and Allyson Longueira, and republished *The Elusive Pimpernel* by Baroness Orczy in a new edition for the WordFire Press Classics collection.

On the weekends, Aisley can be found running, reading, or geeking out about Spider-Man, dinosaurs, and Harry Potter. She loves snuggling her husband and cats, going on camp trips, cooking delicious dinners, and having a good time with friends and family.

For more information on Aisley's upcoming projects, please visit her website at www.aisley oliphant.com/books.

facebook.com/aisleywrites1
instagram.com/aisleywrites

Want updates on future projects?

Sign up for Aisley's monthly newsletter and get Insider perks!

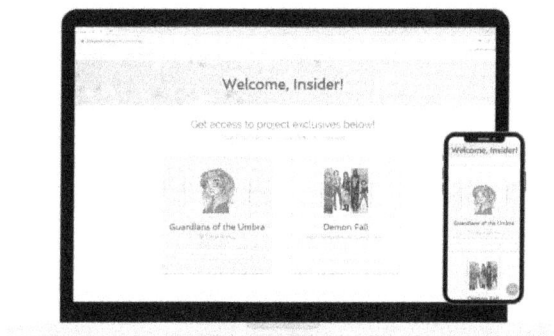

Becoming an Insider gives you access to...

Project Spotify playlists
Character art
Full sample chapters
Project inspiration boards
Cover first looks
FREE printable worksheets
Book news

...and more!

https://www.aisleyoliphant.com/contact

www.ingramcontent.com/pod-product-compliance
Lightning Source LLC
Chambersburg PA
CBHW022103020426
42335CB00012B/805